THE ULTIMATE GUIDE TO SMSF INVESTMENT

How to protect and
safely grow your wealth
via the share market

LUKE CUMMINGS
and
CHAD BURGESS

The Ultimate Guide to SMSF Investment –
How to protect and safely grow your wealth
via the share market

Copyright © 2015 by Luke Cummings and Chad Burgess

First Printing 2015

CONTENTS

FOREWORD

I had just finished an exhausting training session with the Manly Sea Eagles, the NRL club I used to play for, when one of the coaches told us a company was coming to give a talk to the players on how to invest safely in the stock market. The talks were to be in a series over a few weeks and were focused on making consistent returns rather than massive short term windfalls... or at least that is what I understood it to be about at that stage. Investing in the market however was furthest from my mind. All I could think about at that moment was how to beat Parramatta in our upcoming clash.

Like many professional athletes I knew that I wouldn't be playing football forever. The market had always interested me but I had limited experience and, more importantly, limited time to dedicate to managing investments. Learning to trade in such a way that would provide cash flow after I gave up playing rugby league wasn't that big a priority at that time.

But in any case I decided to go along to see what it was all about.

The day came and the whole team was gathered to hear this trader talk about how he'd used the share market to build wealth using low risk trading opportunities. That is when I met Luke Cummings.

When Luke started talking about his values and how he trades he captured our attention. He treated us like humans and not like a money pit. Luke's ability to break down complex strategies to a level where anybody can understand his method is what I still admire today. For someone with limited prior experience to trading I soon started to understand what he was trying to achieve and so too how he'd go about it. It is one of the reasons I ended up trusting him to manage my investments, something he's done ever since.

I also admire Luke's ability to give unbiased advice and his tell-it-how-it-is attitude. Unlike some others I have dealt with Luke doesn't sugar-coat things. As you will see when you read through this book, he always sets realistic expectations. This means that when we have a losing trade (or a series of losing trades) I am always prepared and able to look at things from a longer-term perspective.

Being a high profile sports personality definitely has its perks but it also means that there are a lot of people who are after your money and who may not have your best interest at heart (to say it nicely). His advice in this book on "spotting the salesman" is something I still use today in other areas of my life.

Since Luke and I started working together I have been a significant beneficiary of the takeover strategy that he outlines in this book. One particular trade that sticks in my mind is a trade we did in Centrebet Limited which is still making me money today despite the fact that the trade was closed several years ago. In that specific example, we bought and sold Centrebet shares after they became the subject of a takeover. We made very little on the trade upfront but the key was that taking the trade entitled us to regular distributions over a number of years thereafter as a result of a court case that Centrebet won after the takeover was completed. These payments will continue for years to come and provide me a valuable income stream. Luke's ability to identify opportunities where no one else would even think to look is what makes his advice so valuable.

It's worth noting that when deciding to pursue investing in the stock market I wasn't interested in get rich quick schemes. I had made a good living out of playing professional football and wasn't in need of generating large sums of cash quickly. Instead I was interested in making consistent returns and protecting the capital I did have. This is why the strategies that Luke suggested appealed to me. These are the same strategies that are extensively discussed in this book. It's also why they are perfect for those people who are running a SMSF. I never wanted to wake up one day and see a large portion of my capital gone. As volatility increased throughout 2008, I used takeovers and specific dividend plays to make money no matter what direction the market was headed. That was definitely a relief and one that many investors didn't have the luxury of having.

I haven't had a chance to meet Chad Burgess personally; but knowing Luke well and the fact that he has such high standards in running his business ventures, gives me the confidence to say that he would also know what he is talking about. I would have no hesitation in recommending their new blog The Long and Short of It or Luke's hedge fund 789 Asset Management to any of my friends, family or colleagues.

I hope you enjoy this book

Steve Menzies

Former Manly Sea Eagles,
NSW and Australian NRL representative

INTRODUCTION

Why the hell should I consider a SMSF?

Once bitten?

"Investment": it's a word that doesn't quite have the comforting ring of caution and security it once did. And given the bumpy financial ride we've all had to live through over recent years that should hardly come as a surprise.

Whereas investment might once have seemed like the innately sensible thing to do – the best way to prepare for one's future and to ensure a comfortable retirement – the concept now comes heavily coloured by a newly dominant flavour: risk.

Nowadays the markets can feel like an unsafe place to invest and it's very tempting to look for other solutions.

And of course it makes perfect sense to want to find new ways through this redrawn financial landscape. The 'tech crash' in 2000 gave many people a taste of what was to come and so it's more than likely that when it did eventually hit, the Global Financial Crisis (GFC wasn't their first experience of what can happen to the value of investments when things go horribly wrong.

Albert Einstein once said, "The true definition of madness is repeating the same action, over and over, hoping for a different result." So of course it only stands to reason that if you managed your own SMSF through the tech crash, and then through the tsunami that was the Global Financial Crisis it might feel like madness to continue.

A cure for madness

The purpose of this book is to help you look a bit deeper into the details of managing a SMSF – to help you understand exactly what is and isn't madness – so that you can continue to trade sensibly and securely, and be confident that as you continue to run a SMSF you are not repeating the same action over and over – and that you are not in fact mad.

Because whilst long-term deposits, and the interest they generate, are stable and secure, it's unlikely in the current (and indeed foreseeable) economic climate that they deliver the returns you might have planned for.

Which leaves you looking for a solution that can deliver

the dividends you need, but that doesn't carry the risk of catastrophe that's bitten you in the past.

We think that running a SMSF still offers just such a solution – as long as they are managed with informed and sensible tactics and strategies – and that the only madness you need to cure is in fact needless risk.

And that's why we've written this book - to walk you through those tactics and strategies, so that you can employ them and sleep at night safe in the knowledge that waking up to the news that the overseas markets have fallen significantly won't mean your trading account (and the balance of your super fund) has been blown to smithereens.

How did it ever come to this?

It is of course a story that's now been endlessly retold and anguished over in the intervening years – and understandably so, since it lies at the heart of many investors' hesitation when it comes to running a SMSF.

During the Global Financial Crisis in 2008, investor confidence hit all-time lows. Markets around the world experienced large sell-offs as volatility increased to levels that shocked even the professionals.

A large number of investors ultimately lost a substantial amount of their overall wealth and sadly for many people this included a significant portion of their superannuation.

Our market wasn't excluded from the carnage. From its high in 2007 the Australian market declined 55% to the level at which it eventually bottomed out on the 31 March 2009. The result was that a large number of investors (maybe even you) lost a big portion of their wealth because they weren't positioned for an event of this nature.

Fast forward to today (June 2015), and the market has almost doubled. With that, confidence has returned to the market and investors are looking for safer ways to invest their hard earned money, particularly their superannuation.

The rates available for holding cash are such that investors have little choice but to be invested in shares in some way but the memory of the GFC looms large.

That's why for many investors today the critical question that needs to be answered before re-engaging with shares-based investment is simply this: how can I be confident that my risk will be managed?

But to answer that question, and to create that belief, we must first establish the absolute clarity and thorough comprehension of all the controls investors have over their investments, and which were perhaps lacking in the past.

A bit of perspective

The tech crash in 2000 and the Global Financial Crisis in 2008 are but two examples of extreme market moves that many investors, including the professionals, didn't see coming and a great deal of wealth was destroyed in both instances. They were traumatic events that caused mass migrations of investors from the market.

But it's worth remembering that it doesn't take a market crash for traders to lose money. And nor was that ever in fact the case. The crashes simply taught a large number of people a tough lesson in the most brutal and unforgiving way: that inadequate risk management and lack of preparation for all eventualities can destroy trading accounts irrespective of the state of the general market.

But in learning that lesson the hard way, an important truth has been lost, and that truth is that equity investment is still the most financially rewarding way to invest. So whilst it might have been *easier* to make money in a rising market, it was never actually *easy* – because in rising markets, risks often tend to be overlooked, confidence can rapidly turn into recklessness, and any gains made all too easily lost.

That's why the market can be a scary – and risky – place for those with little to no experience. The excitement of entering a trade can soon turn to fear as one or more of your trades turn sour and you can't figure out whether to sell, hold or buy more.

Back in business

So, if we're so sure the markets are still the place to invest, and running a SMSF is the best option to do so, then what next?

It's quite simple – education. Understanding the risks so that you can avoid them. Being able to differentiate between an opportunity and a gamble.

To become a proficient and consistently profitable trader takes considerable planning and a lot of hard work. If you're not willing to do the required work then trading is simply not for you – because not doing the work exposes you to risk. And as we've already established: that way lies madness.

To trade today's markets effectively you need to allocate time to constantly educate yourself about an environment that is constantly changing.

We now live in a world where we have access to information that is updated and disseminated in real time. With so many ways to trade and so many strategies to utilise it's easy to enter the market but even easier to give up and say "this is just too hard". Many investors did exactly that following the GFC by taking money (or what they had left of it) out of the market and placing it in a term deposit. This may have seemed like a good idea at the time but history tells us it wasn't. Markets have since recovered and the interest rates available on term deposits are at all-time lows. However, for some people the peace of mind of knowing their money is 'safe' outweighs any gains that they are foregoing by not having at least some exposure to the share market. Even if this means that their standard of living in retirement isn't going to be quite what they once envisioned.

It doesn't have to be that way:

- You can become consistently profitable and make returns that exceed the current cash rate while taking limited risk

- You can build confidence by educating yourself

- You can make money regardless of market direction or volatility

- There are strategies that are available to you, that can be easily implemented and they make money (over and over again)!

You won't make money on every trade (that much we can guarantee) but if you follow the advice in this book you can position yourself so that you will be profitable over the long run (and perhaps even straight away).

Why should you trust us?

This book is written by two former stockbrokers who have spent their careers developing low risk strategies that make money with small and infrequent losses.

Luke Cummings is the **Founder and Managing Director of investment blog The Long and Short of It** and the **Chief Investment Officer** of **789 Asset Management. Chad Burgess** is the **Head Analyst at The Long and Short of It** and the main writer of our blog.

As professionals within the industry we have traded personally and on behalf of our clients for over a decade. Most of the money we manage is on behalf of super funds (SMSF's specifically) so it's no coincidence the strategies that we have created are targeted at that area.

Our industry has no shortage of characters (good and bad), a regulatory framework that struggles to keep pace with technology and the (at times misplaced) ingenuity of market participants. On top of this it has a range of vested interests as well as media that provides information (and mis-information) on a 24/7 basis.

Technology enables the average 'man on the street' to trade millions of dollars' worth of financial instruments online with the click of a mouse (and without necessarily having the million dollars in question).

Having seen the good, the bad and the ugly we have noticed that there are a large amount of investors who are comfortable when things are rosy but who aren't equipped to handle things when they turn ugly.

With a growing number of companies claiming that you can double or even triple your trading account with minimal time and effort required, investors these days are fixated on making massive returns. They don't realise that to make these types of returns, they have to take large risks and use leveraged products. More often than not the experience ends in a significant decline in the value of their account and not the increase you were promised when you started trading.

But let's be honest – we have all been in this situation. Everyone starts with limited knowledge of the market, thinks they are bullet proof and then reality sets in. Mistakes are made and they cost you money, sometimes a lot of money. Everyone makes mistakes, including us. The important thing is to learn from those mistakes but also to prepare for them so that when they do happen, the damage to your trading account isn't fatal. Overconfidence and position sizes that are too big are a fast road to ruin. Rigorous research, a healthy dose of scepticism and appropriate risk management however, give you more than a fighting chance.

The truth is that the industry has become overrun with sales men (and women) posing as traders. These people rarely trade themselves and are more interested in making money off you via transactional revenue than putting their own money on the line and backing their own advice.

We have spent our entire careers refining our methods with real money. Sometimes that meant looking in places that other people might not to find an opportunity, but most of the time we looked where everyone else was looking and took trades to make a return that no one else was interested in. That might be a return that "will only make 3% over 3 months."

We have found that most investors neglect these types of returns because the "returns aren't big enough". But these same people have money in a standard bank account that is earning less than 3% for the entire year! One of the key lessons we have learned over the years is to never discount the power of compounding returns.

We will explore that concept in more detail a little later on.

We are writing this book so that you can benefit from the experience we have gained over many years. You will:

- Learn what to look for in a broker

- Decide what type of trader/investor you want to be

- Find out the pros and cons of trading as an individual or as a company, trust or via a SMSF

- Develop confidence in the market

- Realise there are ways to make money and reduce risk without betting on a market direction

- Find out what a typical day in our life looks like when we run you through exactly what we do on a daily basis in order to find trades and also to manage our existing ones.

Everyone from Warren Buffett down has been burnt by the market and at times lost confidence in their ability to successfully invest in the stock market. Some have been burnt more than others. Our aim is that by the time you have finished reading this book you will have significantly reduced the possibility of this happening again (if you've been burnt before) or at all (if you're fortunate enough to have not had a negative experience previously.

If you are running a SMSF or thinking about running one in the future, we think our book is a must read.

CHAPTER 1

Getting started – setting up to succeed

Introduction

As with all successful business ventures, the value of the preparatory work you do *before* you actually start up can be make or break for you in terms of success. No bank would invest in a business that didn't have a rigorous business plan in place, with all the moving parts clearly defined alongside sensible pathways to successful returns on that investment – and nor should you.

And it that sense, setting up a SMSF is no different to setting up a business. So the first thing to do is to simply stop; think and plan. Only then can you be confident that the investment path you are plotting will actually get you to where you want to go.

In this chapter we will explore in some depth the five key considerations that we believe are essential for you to think about before you do anything:

1. **Choosing the right broker**
    Does the broker you have chosen to work with understand your goals, know how to achieve them and, perhaps most importantly, are they worth the money they cost?

2. **Are you a trader or investor?**
    There are different ways to play the "game", with the day-trade approach at one end of the spectrum, long-term investment at the other, and everything else in between. You will need to know where on that spectrum you plan to do business.

3. **Spotting the salesman**
    It's a competitive environment with big potential wins to be had but also, as discussed in the introduction, big potential losses. The key to successfully navigating risk in this environment means knowing who to trust, and whose advice you should take with a healthy pinch of salt.

4. **Setting up the right account**
    Depending on the nature of the trade(s) you are planning, the estimated holding period(s) and the funds required, you will need to understand the

pros and cons of executing all of your trades within your SMSF versus also trading as an individual or via a company or trust.

5. **Do software programs mean success?**

    If they did, wouldn't everyone always use them and always succeed? Software can *help*, but how much depends on you, how you plan to approach the market and the specific data you need. There is no such thing as plug-and-play success.

1.1 Choosing the right broker

Won't any old broker do?

Short answer: no.

Whether you're just starting out running a SMSF, or if you have already started trading, it is important that you find the right broker for YOU.

But what exactly does that mean?

It involves asking yourself the following:

- Do you need a full service broker or are you confident trading through an online broker by yourself?

- What brokerage charges can you afford to pay

without compromising the profitability of your trading system?

- What other services do you need to further your knowledge? and

- If you do need a full service broker, how good is the service they are providing?

The answers to these questions will depend heavily on your experience level but finding the right mix can significantly help your trading.

How?

If you are new to the market you may have no experience and a full service broker can be your best friend. But you do need to make sure that they have your best interests in mind (see next section) and are not just trying to increase their own pay packet. Remember it's your super that's at stake and that's not something you want to take lightly.

What to expect of a broker

The role of a full service broker is to <u>support</u> you. They help you place trades, they offer recommendations and they can act as a sounding board for any ideas of your own.

In return for this support, they will more than likely charge a higher brokerage rate to compensate for the time they are spending with you. This rate can vary from 0.5% to over 1%

of the value of each trade depending on the level of skill and experience they have.

Ultimately their job is to make you money, or to help you to do so. If they aren't doing that then you should seriously consider whether the service they are providing is worth the increased amount they are charging you.

However, if they are providing a valuable service a newbie can find their help to be priceless. The following example will show you why.

Suppose you want to place a trade to purchase 3,000 shares in a listed company, let's say it's Magellan Financial Group Limited (ASX Code: MFG). If you are new to the market you probably don't know how to use different order types[1] or know how market depth[2] works but bare with us.

Most people don't have the time to sit in front of a computer and watch the market all day as they have other commitments. If you are one of those people and you are placing your orders to buy and sell shares online you might use a market order[3] to purchase the shares quickly. Using a market order

---

1   A trade order is an instruction that is sent to a broker to enter or exit a position.

2   Market depth is a snapshot of all buyers and sellers for a particular stock at a given point in time.

3   A market order is an order to buy or sell a stock at the best currently available price.

basically guarantees that your order is filled immediately but not necessarily at the best price.

After you place the market order to buy MFG you immediately buy 500 shares at $17.72, 800 shares at $17.85 and 1700 shares at $17.92. This means that you have purchased 3000 shares for a total of $53,604 excluding brokerage (which in this instance we would expect to be approximately 0.1% of the trade value or $53.52).

So how would a broker save money?

Now suppose you used a full service broker to place the same order.

They should know that the MFG market depth is quite illiquid and usually there is a large gap between the first buyer in the queue who is willing to purchase shares at the highest price and the first seller in the queue who is willing to sell their shares at the lowest price. As a result they use their experience to place a limit order[4] to buy the 3,000 shares at a maximum price of $17.65. If they are successful they will buy you 3,000 shares for a total of $52,950. Although they will most likely charge you a higher brokerage fee they have effectively saved you money as they have reduced your entry price into the stock by $654. Even if they charge you 1%

---

4   A limit order is an order to buy or sell a set number of shares at a specified price or better.

($529.50 in this instance) you will still come out in front (by $124.50) and it only gets better if they charge less than 1%.

Of course the full service broker's skill and experience will determine his ability to save you money. If they aren't very good they may actually cost you more money than they save/make you, so you need to be careful and make sure they have been in the market for a reasonable period of time and more importantly that they know what they are doing.

Another benefit of using a full service broker may be that you can obtain access to IPO's, discounted placements and other opportunities which are offered exclusively via that broker and are not widely available to the general public. Once again, some brokers will be better at this than others but for access to the right opportunities, paying a little extra in commissions can be well worth it.

Know what you're doing? Then perhaps an online broker...

It might however be the case that you are already fairly experienced in the markets and trade regularly. Your system might produce a lot of signals and a brokerage rate of 1% per trade may be too much in order for your system to remain profitable. In this case you would definitely want to open an account with an online broker. That way, you are saving money on brokerage and only using the services you need i.e. the ability to place trades quickly and inexpensively.

In this case you should spend your time comparing the brokerage rate and trading platforms of the different online brokers to determine which one is most likely to suit your needs.

Your profitability can increase by choosing the right broker. Determining exactly what you need is something you need to consider before you start trading in your SMSF and one that many people (surprisingly) rarely think about.

1.2 Do you want to be a trader or investor?

Never mind the funds - how much time do you have to invest?

Before you start trading away with your retirement funds it is good to have an idea of what sort of trader you want to be. If you've already placed your first trade then now is still a good time to reassess!

By this I mean do you want to be a day trader? A swing trader (typically holding positions between 1 and 5 days)? A medium term investor? Or maybe a long term investor? It is also a good idea to check that whichever option you choose is allowed as per the mandate of your SMSF trust deed. If your deed nominates that the fund is a long term 'buy and hold' investor then day trading probably isn't going to be an option. You'll either need to adjust your approach or else have your trust deed amended to cater to your intended trading style.

The time you have available to trade the market will play a big part in your decision as will your previous experience in the markets. There is no point saying you want to be a day trader if you have to work full time and are not able to sit in front of a screen watching the price action of the market for long periods of time.

Different ways to trade

Day traders need the time to dedicate solely to trading and to be in an environment with little or no distractions. This type of trading can be very rewarding but at the same time it can be very boring and the slightest distraction can be deadly to your bottom line via missed opportunities or mistakes caused by a lack of attention. In our opinion this is the hardest type of trading and not one to begin with if you have had no exposure to trading in the past. It's also not generally an approach that we'd recommend that you employ for a super fund (but hey, it is your money).

If you have had some experience and decide that you want to try day trading then you also need to work out what charting timeframe you will use. Will you use a 3-minute chart? A 15-minute chart? A 4-hour chart? This will ultimately determine how active you are throughout the day. Generally the longer the timeframe, the less active you will be.

A safer option would be to start off investing in (or trading) medium to longer term positions so that you can get a feel for how the market works.

Through our trading career we have traded almost every style known to man. We have day traded and swing traded and found that each style suited both of us differently.

What works for one person may not necessarily work for another and because of that you must work out what works best for you.

How analysis informs the way you trade

What may help you in determining how often to trade is whether you will use technical or fundamental analysis.

Fundamental analysis uses financial ratios (typically gleaned from a company's financial reports) to determine the viability of an investment in that particular security. Technical analysis uses price data, including indicators such as moving averages, to catch trends and find stocks where the price is likely to move in a preferred particular direction.

Both methods have their merits and both have been used by a large number of investors and top traders to make consistent profits. You can use either method or a combination of both in creating your system but which one you choose will once again determine how often you trade. Fundamental analysis is generally used for medium to long term investing whereas technical analysis is generally used for short to medium term trading.

Using fundamental analysis to day trade is pretty much

impossible. The flow of financial information is not updated fast enough to allow you to make informed decisions on an intra-day basis. Therefore, those who day trade rely heavily on price action and the psychology of the market to make a profit.

On the flipside you generally have to look at a company's financial statements and research what they do to assess whether the company will do well into the future. Therefore, if you are a long term investor it is hard to ignore fundamental analysis when choosing where/how to allocate your money on a longer term basis.

Creating your trading system

The indicators to use and how to use them to create a system is unfortunately beyond the scope of this book. There is however a wealth of information available online to help you create a system that suits you.

You may even want to purchase a software program to back test some ideas and/or use a market scanning program to forward test potential future trades. These both have their limitations and you may again want to consult online resources for further help in this area.

But if you would like to talk to someone who has considerable experience in trading systems development then we can happily recommend Share Wealth Systems. Founder, Gary Stone and the SWS team have been creating and testing trading systems for many years. They are particularly well suited to the super fund space and deal with many clients who run their own SMSF. In our opinion they are worth a call to discuss system development and they also have some mighty fine software that can be of assistance in that regard. You can find their contact details on their website if you are interested in talking to them.

So, what instruments should you trade?

And as if all of that isn't enough to think about, you also need to decide what instruments to trade. In today's world there are so many instruments it's hard to choose just one. You can trade shares, bonds, futures, options, foreign exchange (FX), warrants or even CFD's. Each have their own advantages and disadvantages and it is important to know exactly how they work before trading them. Again, at this point you must make sure that your SMSF mandate allows you to trade the instruments that you are considering. For example, there is no use wanting to trade leveraged products if your SMSF mandate prohibits trading in those products (which will frequently be the case).

If you are new to the market then you may want to start with trading shares before venturing off to some of the more complex alternatives. Shares are arguably the easiest to understand and a good place to gain experience before venturing further afield.

There is actually no reason you cannot be both a trader and an investor at the same time. Ultimately though, you should choose whatever you feel comfortable with and that will typically be those products or instruments that you have the most knowledge about. Having extensive knowledge of how multiple instruments work and how they affect one another can improve your ability to spot opportunities in the market. This will come more naturally as you gain experience.

1.3 Spotting the salesman

Unfortunately the number of people who give financial advice and actually successfully trade themselves is outweighed heavily by those who have a sales mindset and are only in it for personal gain (which generally involves doing as little of their own trading as possible and for good reason – whilst they are happy to lose your money they are not generally as happy about losing their own). Thankfully that is starting to slowly change as the industry adopts a better model.

You should be very careful when taking financial advice from someone you don't know well, in particular with regard to your SMSF given that you are essentially trusting them with your future livelihood. When searching for a broker or adviser I'd almost treat the process like a job interview and ask as many questions as possible.

You really need to cut through the sales spin and determine if they can actually make you real money and not just false promises. I can't stress this point enough. The number of sales people in the finance industry that will try and sell you the dream is ever increasing. That these people can be called 'Financial Advisors' when they are simply glorified sales people is laughable. You need to make sure that you are not their next victim!

The first question I would ask someone who I'm considering taking advice from is "do you have any historical results that you can send me that have been traded with real money". It is important to emphasise and confirm that the results are from trades using real money and not simulated results where real money is not on the line.

We could easily produce a year, 2 years or even 5 years' worth of results that are based on 'simulated data' and smash it out of the park. It is a lot more difficult to prove you are consistently profitable using real money mostly because you can't manipulate the data i.e. you either made money or you didn't.

Additionally, the more that someone can tell you about how they are choosing their trades the better. Some traders may want to keep the specific details under wraps but they should be able to at least give you some idea of how they go about identifying trades.

At The Long and Short of It we have no issues sharing with our subscribers our reasons for getting into (or out of) a trade and we do that in order to be as transparent as possible. Firstly, we think we have a pretty great system and we want people to know about it. We also believe that this level of openness helps people to understand the inherent risks involved with our system.

When a trade doesn't work out (as will inevitably be the case from time to time) we don't want that to be a surprise to anyone, so preparing our subscribers for that possibility is very important to us.

Another question I would also ask a prospective service provider is how many years they have been trading their system for. The longer the better!

Ideally, the system will also have been traded through a variety of market conditions. Generally, it's much more difficult to make money in a market that's going down than it is to make money in a market that's going up (because most systems have an overwhelming long bias meaning that they generate trades that involve being long rather than short). Of course, past performance is not a guarantee of future performance but it's a good place to start.

The market can (and does) change but a good trader can generally adapt. That's not to say they'll make money in all market conditions but ideally a system should work in all types of markets and/or (more likely) a trader should have a number of systems that they can implement such that if one system is not effective in current market conditions then an alternate system that is better suited to current conditions can be employed.

We would also be using the history provided to determine

the variability of returns. Some very profitable systems are subject to periods of significant draw down (i.e. losses). Good ultimate performance is of little consolation if you can't handle the variability of returns in the interim period.

Arguably the most important question of all is how they protect their capital and how much portfolio capital they risk on each trade. It's all very well if they are making 60-70% per annum but if they are doing it by risking 20% of your capital in each trade then your account may not last long enough for you to enjoy the benefit of those returns.

Risk management in the form of downside protection is in our opinion the most important component of any system and it's therefore very important that any person or company that you entrust your capital to has adequate risk management measures in place. In fact, the extent to which rigorous risk management is absent is often the quickest way to spot a cowboy.

A number of very large companies who manage billions of dollars have failed because of inadequate risk measures. To give you one example, in mid-January 2015 the Swiss National Bank un-pegged its currency to the Euro. What this means is that it essentially removed the 1.20 Euro cap and let the Swiss Franc trade freely against the Euro.

As a result of this decision the Everest Capital Global Fund lost almost all of its money as it had large positions that were bearish on the Swiss currency. Unfortunately for them the announcement made by the Swiss National Bank caused the Swiss Franc to rally hard against many of its fellow currencies, something they definitely didn't want to happen.

Now this wasn't a small fund. It had about $830 million in assets at the end of 2014 and it had been through 5 separate emerging market debt crises in its 24 year life so their founders weren't newbies to the game. They obviously had too much exposure to this currency and it's a prime example of how important risk management is even when an event seems very unlikely to occur.

If practical, another good idea (but not essential) is to try and meet the person you'll be entrusting your capital to face to face. You can generally get a much better feel for someone in person. Beware though of anyone that dodges questions or seems like they have something to hide (whether in person or otherwise).

We have seen far too many traders give money to a broker only to come back 6 months later and see that 50% of their capital is gone.

In no way am I saying all brokers are bad and you should blame them for their results. We have always been of the belief that you should take responsibility for your own actions and even if you have given money to a broker, adviser or hedge fund you should always take an active approach and monitor what they are doing on a regular and consistent basis. Failure to do so and then to later blame them when your capital disappears won't get your money back and it definitely won't improve your skill level or your knowledge of the market.

Ultimately, when choosing a financial services provider the more questions you can ask the better. There is still no guarantee that you'll choose the best provider possible but it will significantly improve your chances of avoiding a bad one. Failure to do so may result in you losing a large amount of your superannuation and mean that you need to keep working well after you planned on retiring.

Unfortunately there is no set formula for distinguishing between a salesman and a genuine trader that will provide a benefit to your trading. In most cases you need to go with your gut feel. If something feels off then it probably is.

1.4 Setting up the right account

The advantages and disadvantages of trading via a SMSF

When setting up a SMSF it is worth considering how trading under this structure will differ to trading in a company name, via a trust (excluding a SMSF) or in your individual name.

Do you know the advantages and disadvantages of trading via a SMSF compared to the following structures?

- Company
- Trust
- Individual name

Obviously if you are planning on trading with your super money then you need to trade via a SMSF structure. Knowing the advantages and disadvantages of the other types of trading accounts may help you determine what account will give you the best outcome (and it may not be a SMSF after all).

Many of the advantages and disadvantages are tax related and because of that you really do need to talk to your tax adviser and/or accountant so that they can give you advice that is specific to your personal situation (something which we cannot do).

Trading in a personal name

Trading in a personal name is the most common structure for a beginner. In terms of setting up an account it is also the easiest. All you usually need to do is complete an application form and provide some certified ID.

If you are on a zero tax rate, trades such as those that include fully franked dividends are best suited to an individual account (unless you are in the pension phase of your super fund in which case you should gain the same benefit doing the trade through your SMSF).

A non-working spouse trading in their name under an individual account structure can be an effective way to maximise profits. If they have also invested in companies that pay fully franked dividends they may also be eligible for a tax credit (thereby further enhancing returns). More on that later.

The way that taxation laws are structured in Australia means that one thing to consider when deciding on what structure is best suited to you is the likely frequency of your trading. If you hold a trade for longer than 12 months, you are generally entitled to a 50% discount on the assessable capital gain that you need to pay tax on.

What this means is that if you close out a trade that you have held for longer than 12 months and you make a profit of $500, you only need to pay tax on $250 of that at your personal tax rate and not the full $500 gain. This rule is only available to individual and trust accounts (where income is ultimately distributed to an individual). A SMSF qualifies for a smaller 33% CGT discount for investments held for 12 months or more.

So why is this important?

If you are a short term investor and close trades out regularly then you won't be eligible for this concession in any structure.

On a very basic level, one of the primary points to consider when choosing the structure that will best suit your personal situation is which tax bracket you fall into for income tax purposes.

If you fall into a tax bracket that is below the company tax rate of 30% then trading in an individual name and possibly trading via a trust account (including a SMSF) will likely be your best options.

Trading as a company or a trust

If however your tax rate is greater than the company tax rate of 30% you may find it more beneficial to trade under a company structure as opposed to trading as an individual.

Where it gets a bit tricky is when you're choosing to trade in either a company or a trust account. It becomes even trickier when deciding whether you choose to make an individual or company the trustee of your SMSF.

Confused?

Don't worry, this is why it is important to talk to an accountant who can give you professional advice in this area. The most important consideration to take away with you is that this is an area that requires some consideration. We personally use a variety of accounts (individual, company, trust and SMSF) to trade with. The actual entity for which each trade is executed is determined by the nature of the trade, the estimated holding period and the funds required.

1.5 Do software programs mean success?

Even the best software can make losses

When new traders enter the market they often think that if they use the best charting package available there is no chance they could ever lose money.

We can tell you that isn't true. We know because we were

once upon a time guilty of thinking the same thing. When we started out, we would close a trade that lost money and think if only we had this indicator or that indicator we would surely become profitable. We were wrong!

Sure charting programs help and they can improve your profitability to some extent but if your system isn't profitable to begin with then it won't matter if you have the functionality to do back testing, market scanning or access each and every technical indicator under the sun. You still won't make money.

For those who use technical analysis, a good charting package can help. It will allow you to trade your system using the indicators you have chosen.

Before deciding to buy that charting program that you have been looking at let us ask you a couple of questions.

Do you currently use custom indicators that you have created yourself?

If the answer is no then a simple charting package should provide everything that you will need.

Are you new to the market?

If the answer is yes then most of the online brokers provide platforms which will do way more than what you need.

In most cases the only thing purchasing an expensive charting package will do is cost you money and waste capital you could otherwise be using to make money placing actual trades!

Simplicity beats complexity

Remember, you don't have to use a large number of complex indicators to make money. Even simple systems like purchasing a stock after it hits support (as an example) can be all you need to make money in the market. Having a large number of rules can give you conflicting signals, confuse you and make it easier to make mistakes. The crucial thing is to trade your system flawlessly and without error!

Think about it for a second. If you are a day trader and have 2 separate systems one with 20 rules and another with just 3 rules which do you think will be easier to trade quickly without error? A software package might assist you in this case and make the system with 20 rules just as easy to implement but again it comes down to if the system makes money already (because the software itself certainly isn't likely to).

To use an analogy, Daniel Riccardo is a good driver irrespective of whether he's driving a Vauxhall Astra (as Top Gear shows) or an F1 car. The F1 car allows him to further leverage his talents but he was a good driver to begin with. For someone who has never driven a car before, neither a Vauxhall Astra nor an F1 car will help them but the Vauxhall Astra is likely to be safer at the outset and a whole lot less expensive to fix if something goes wrong.

Buying the right data

Here is a big tip that will save you a lot of money!

When you open an account with an online broker they will most likely include static data with the package. This is price data that only gives you the prices at that immediate point in time. It won't refresh automatically like real time tick data will.

If you trade intraday or like to "time" your entry and exits then you may want to upgrade to real time tick data. This is data that updates automatically and allows you to monitor movements in a company's share price intraday. Usually this costs around $30 a month.

Some brokers such as E*TRADE have professional programs to access this data. E*TRADE Pro offers real time data and news functionality. It costs $80 a month but you also get that amount rebated if you do a certain amount of trades each month. If you are an active trader it therefore pays to research what deals are on offer to you as a client. You may find a better deal that saves you money (i.e. trading capital) in the long run.

A large majority of those traders managing their SMSF will trade based on a longer time frame and will do just fine with the static data. Although $30 a month doesn't sound like much, if you have a small account balance of $5,000 (hopefully you will have more than that if you are trading in a SMSF) you're wasting 7.2% of your trading capital per year in data fees alone.

This means that you will need to return 7.2% p.a. to break even. For someone who is new to the market it's hard enough to finish the year in the profit without the added pressure of unnecessary costs.

Learn to walk before you try to run

There is a different scenario whereby you may become successful if you use a software program. You could purchase a mechanical trading system (a 'self-driving car' if you like that has been proven to be consistently profitable over a long period of time and you trade it according to its rules without error.

We would however argue that although the software does contribute to your success in trading, your personality has a lot to do with your ability to trade the system efficiently. We have seen traders use software programs that provide buy and sell signals which have been profitable over the long term only to still lose money. This is because they try to improve an already profitable system by picking which trades to do and which ones to ignore.

We would suggest that if you are going to purchase a black box trading system you trade it the way it was intended. If you don't, you will never know if the system actually works or if the reason you're losing money is not because of the system but because you think you're better than its creators. You may ultimately find out that you can improve upon the system but failing to adhere to it in the early days isn't generally the way to go about it.

CHAPTER 2

Doing the work – getting the job done

Introduction

So you've put the plan together. You have a clear idea now of what you hope to achieve, who you're planning to work with (and who you intend to avoid) to achieve it, and what software and kit you plan to use once you're up and running.

It's time now to get on and do the work. As with all best laid plans, they just love to go astray but that is the nature of the beast: if there were no variables, there would be no gains to be had (and indeed no losses to beware of), so the whole thing would be a pointless exercise.

So, as with getting set up, and making that plan, there are now some key parameters that would be very sensible to define to ensure you don't deviate from your long-term goals, however such short-term variables and changes might unnerve you. In this chapter we will look at those three key parameters for doing the work:

1. **Can you afford to lose?**

   No matter what sort of system you have, it's very likely that you will experience losses. But how will you differentiate between an acceptable loss, and a loss that means it's time to reassess the system and/or your goals?

2. **Putting in the time**

   If you don't have the time to trade a system, you will need to find someone who can trade it for you. Not allocating enough time to a system will waste your time, money and seriously affect your profitability.

3. **Risking the right amount**

   You have a certain amount available to invest – but have you factored in education and brokerage costs? You need to strike the right balance between caution (education and brokerage) and risk (investment) to ensure that you see the growth you need.

2.1 Can you afford to lose?

Don't Panic! Every system can make a loss...

You will rarely come across a system that works all the time. Dr Van Tharp, a very well-known trading coach who specialises in trading psychology believes that there are different types of markets and you cannot build a mechanical system that works in all of them. Whether you agree with that will depend on your beliefs about the market.

In our case we believe that may be true if you are trading a purely mechanical system but if you trade a system that is market neutral (meaning that the outcome is not dependent on market direction) then things are a little different. Some of our favourite market neutral strategies are outlined later in this book.

No matter what sort of system you have, if you trade that system consistently it's likely that you will experience periods of drawdown i.e. a string of losses. At this time it may be helpful if you have a figure in mind whereby if reached, you will stop trading and reassess the system and/or your goals.

Say you have a SMSF account with $250,000 in cash. What figure could it get down to before you start to question your trading system? $200,000? $100,000?

You should be aware that if you lose 50% of your capital then you need to make a 100% return thereafter just to break even.

Lose 90% and the return needed to break-even skyrockets to 1000%. We don't know about you but if we were to make a 1000% return, we would want it to be a profit and not simply a means to recoup our losses!

Some trend following systems have been proven to be very profitable over the long term but experience drawdowns of up to 80%. Would you be able to withstand 80% of your superannuation disappearing and keep believing in the system? Few traders can!

The challenge is in figuring out if you should stop trading because your system is no longer working or if the drawdown you're experiencing is temporary in nature and merely part of the ebbs and flows of trading your system.

System testing and defining limits

Testing the system via back testing can help you determine the historical maximum drawdown levels but these results should only be used as a guide and not taken as concrete evidence. This is where understanding your risk tolerance and as well as the amount you are willing to lose before you call it quits is important.

If you have a pre-determined level at which you intend to stop trading then when that level is hit (irrespective of the cause) that is your signal to retreat to the sidelines in order to better assess whether to continue with your current system, to work on refining it or to discard it altogether.

As a general rule, you should never invest money into the market that you cannot afford to lose. Doing so may force you to adopt a gamblers mindset and double your risk in order for you to make back the money you've just lost. That can be disastrous for those trading a SMSF (or any account for that matter) and can add enormous pressure to your mindset not to mention extending your working life if things get really bad.

2.2 Putting in the time

Determining how much time you will invest

Before considering the use of someone else's system or purchasing a black box software program to trade in your SMSF you need to sit down and determine just how much time you have available to trade.

It's no use purchasing a day trading program that gives you intraday signals if you're a fulltime landscaper (or better still on the golf course 4 days per week) and can't sit in front of a computer all day. Doing so would be a poor use of your capital and frankly a waste of money.

In Chad's last job, his firm supported a company who sold mechanical trading systems. This would produce end of day signals specifying when to buy and when to sell particular stocks. He provided trading support to those clients who used the system software. Many of his clients were using super fund accounts.

He also offered a service whereby the client could deposit money into an account and he traded the system for them. He did this because some clients wanted to trade the system but didn't have the time available to do it themselves. In addition to the time required, some people simply found it difficult to follow the system without trading outside the rules. They realised this only <u>after</u> they spent quite a bit of money on the software! If not for the service he offered whereby he would implement the system for them, these people would have effectively purchased a system that they did not realistically have the ability to implement.

If they had seriously considered the amount of time they had to commit to their trading they could have saved that money and used it for something more beneficial.

How The Long and Short of It can help

The Long and Short of It is a little different to the norm. We gladly share our strategies for free. Some of them are listed in chapter 3 and you can find free copies of our strategy document online which examines actual examples of how we trade and what we look for. You're free to try and use this system yourself and may be able to do so successfully without our help.

What we trade is not a secret and many High Net Worth individuals are already trading the opportunities that we trade either with or without our help.

We believe that although our subscribers could identify the trades themselves that they will still subscribe to our newsletter and use our experience in the field to their advantage (many subscribers have told us they do exactly that).

Ultimately, to trade our system unassisted you need to ask yourself: do you really have the time and energy to sift through the 100's of company announcements every week to find the next potential trade?

Alternatively, why not let us do all the hard work in exchange for a relatively low subscription cost, leaving you free to enjoy your hard-earned down time?

The fact is that it takes hours upon hours to sift through the large number of company announcements that are presented to us on a daily basis (and which we share with our subscribers in a concise trade notification via email and SMS). Fortunately for us, and also for you, we have the infrastructure in place and the use of a full time IT resource (in the form of a very good programmer) such that we can build tools to identify these opportunities quickly.

In summary, before committing to trading any system you need to understand how much time you need to commit to the system you are intending to trade before you decide to trade it or else you may as well throw money out into the street.

This is a critical consideration. If you don't have the time, then don't trade the system or else find someone who can trade it for you. Failure to allocate enough time to a system will waste your time, money and seriously affect your profitability.

2.3 Risking the right amount

Balancing theory and practice

Even more important than knowing how much time you have is making sure that you have the right risk controls in place so that your account isn't reduced to zero before you even have a chance to make a profit.

Another company that we both used to work for was owned by a trade recommendation service provider who also offered education services (effectively teaching people to trade). Clients who either subscribed to that recommendation service and/or attended the education events would typically open an account with the brokerage division (that we worked for) in order to execute trades.

What astounded us was the number of people who would pay as much as $10,000 for education and the various recommendation services thereby leaving them with less than $5,000 to actually trade with.

Don't get us wrong, you can start investing with $5,000 (although probably not in a SMSF due to the initial setup and ongoing costs). However, in our experience (and we have seen a lot of people try) if you try and trade frequently with a low amount of capital you're likely to end up losing a large portion of this money. That is simply because the number of shares you are trading will be so small that even when you do make a profit the effect of brokerage will eat most or all of it.

Putting the right controls in place

To compensate for this, most people increase the risk they're taking (above and beyond what is recommended by the system) and they lose all of their money that way instead.

Education and trading advice can be a very helpful tool in becoming a profitable trader but if you're using more than half your available funds on education and advice you'll have very little left to actually trade with thereby rendering that education and trade advice useless.

It is important to be realistic and have a look at the recommended minimum starting capital for any system that you intend to trade.

At the Long and Short of It we use a model portfolio of $250,000 and generally risk no more than 2% of that amount on each individual trade. This is mainly because we are targeted at the SMSF space but also because we know that is what works best for the strategies we use. Although you could trade our recommendations with as little as $25,000 (1/10th of the size of our model portfolio), realistically you will find it hard to make money. This is even more evident in trades that we believe carry more risk and therefore suggest risking less than 2% of portfolio capital on the trade.

Following our system with a balance of $250,000 means that by risking a full 2% of your portfolio you are putting $5,000 at risk in each of our trades. If we think that there is more risk in a position but that a successful outcome would more than compensate for the risk of taking the trade then we may suggest risking as little as 0.5% of your portfolio capital on the trade. In this case you are still risking $1,250 and it should result in a sufficient profit amount (in the event of a successful outcome) to make the trade worthwhile. That probably can't be said if you are risking 0.5% of $25,000 i.e. $125.

When considering a potential system to follow you should seriously consider the above points and determine the likelihood of you being profitable with the amount that you have available to trade with. A salesman will always try and convince you that you will be able to make money but if the numbers don't stack up when you do your own calculations then you should be suspicious of their motives.

NB: For the record we'd be comfortable with you following our LASOI recommendations with a portfolio size of as little as $50k and ideally closer to $100k.

CHAPTER 3

Strategies that work

Introduction

If you've made it this far then you're obviously serious about improving your trading. You've taken on board how vital it is to put a plan together. You've looked at building some rigorous structure into the hours you're going to put in and you've also looked at the risks you're prepared to take.

You should now have a clearer understanding of the kind of commitments you need to make to trade successfully and securely in your SMSF.

Time now to look at some of the more detailed strategies you can employ to maximise your returns and truly nurture your investment:

1. **The art of compounding**

   If used correctly the compounding of returns has the potential to quickly turn relatively small SMSF accounts to large accounts: by increasing the frequency of "smaller" returns you often make more money than less frequent large returns.

2. **Trading Takeovers to become market neutral**

   Purchasing a stock that is already under takeover (NB <u>not</u> buying a company in the hope of a takeover, but one where a takeover has already been announced) can enjoy rapid higher bids and reduced exposure to market volatility.

3. **Buy-backs**

   When a company wants to return excess capital to its shareholders it may do so via a share buy-back, which can result in shareholders receiving a better after tax outcome than if they sold their shares on market – an opportunity you don't want to miss.

4. **Dividends/franking credits**

   Franking credits – typically of most benefit to those on a tax rate lower than 30% when they buy shares in a company that pays fully franked dividends. These dividends have already been taxed at the Australian company tax rate of 30% and are the closest thing to a 'free lunch' you're likely to find in the financial markets.

3.1 The art of compounding

Little and often

We believe that the compounding of returns is the single biggest element of trading that is misunderstood by many traders. If used correctly, it has the potential to turn relatively small SMSF accounts to large accounts rather quickly.

What we have found over the years is that traders and investors focus too much on the absolute return on offer for a particular trade or investment and neglect to focus on the frequency with which those absolute returns can be generated. They are hell-bent on holding a stock for 1, 2 or 5 years to make a 30% return but in doing so miss the 50 lower risk (and lower absolute return) trades that could have made them over 100% in aggregate.

What would you say if we told you that you should do a trade and that trade has a potential to make 3% over the next 2 months?

We think that the majority of people out there probably wouldn't be interested as "the return is too small to worry about". They would be partially correct in that the return is certainly small but they would be wrong to believe that the return is not worth worrying about.

If you increase the frequency of these "smaller" returns you have a good chance of making far more money than a less frequent large return will ever provide. As briefly mentioned earlier, if you are in the pension phase of your super fund and pay <u>no tax</u> on earnings you would be stupid to ignore trades of this nature.

Do the math...

Let us give you a simple example to show you why you should be paying more attention to these low returns and how you can use them to make a lot more money than you thought.

Say you have 2 traders each with $100,000 in a trading account. Trader 1 places a trade and makes a return of 25% over a 3 year period. Trader 2 places 8 trades that make the following returns 3%, 4%, 3%, 2%, 2%, 3%, 4%, 2% over the same 3 year period.

Which one do you think had the biggest return (assume both are net of fees)?

If you said Trader 1 you would be incorrect. If you add up the returns of Trader 2 they total 23% (which is less than that of Trader 1) however, straight addition ignores the effect of compounding.

This means that after Trader 2 makes his first profit of 3% he has a balance of $103,000 ((100,000 x 0.03 +100,000, after trade 2 he has $107,120. After all 8 trades he has a final balance of $125,420.35, $420.35 more than trader 1.

Ok so a difference of $420.35 is not a massive deal but suppose you made a 2% return every week for a year and that these trades have a high probability of success.

If you started with $250,000 then at the end of the year you would have over $700,000! This is from a return that, on an individual basis, most people think is "too small for them to worry about".

Now granted we are assuming that you invest the total amount in 1 trade which may be unlikely in your situation. The point we are trying to make however, is that most investors are after massive returns and neglect high probability trades with small returns. In our opinion those doing this are neglecting one of the easiest ways to make money in the market. Trades of this nature are perfect for safely increasing the value of your SMSF.

3.2 Trading Takeovers to become market neutral

One of the best low-risk strategies

It's no secret that we trade takeovers and other corporate events at The Long and Short of It and that these trades feature heavily in the members section of our blog. In our opinion, when traded correctly this is one of the best low risk strategies that you can use in your SMSF and if you're not currently doing it, you should be.

Everyone is aware when a large company is bid for by a

competitor. The media is usually all over it in a (news)flash but what isn't usually covered in any detail are the less obvious terms that govern these deals.

To find them you often need to read the offer document which is sometimes 100's of pages in length and far too boring for most people's liking.

Basically, our strategy involves purchasing a stock that is already under takeover. Note that we are not buying a company in the hope of a takeover emerging at some point in the future but rather buying one where a takeover has already been announced.

We do this in the hope of a higher bid emerging either from one or more additional bidders or courtesy of the initial bidder who improves their bid because the first version received little support from the target company board and/ or major shareholders.

A trade with added benefits

The bid, if we are lucky may also include benefits such as fully franked special dividends or other capital return payments that are a part of the deal but not necessarily immediately obvious.

In most cases, our initial stock purchase is made at a small discount to the bid price but we may also pay a slight premium depending on what we think the probability of a higher bid is. These opportunities are attractive because we are effectively buying a relatively cheap call option over an improved bid. These opportunities also have the benefit of often being too small in size for most big brokers and fund managers to worry about meaning they are readily available to smaller investors.

Of course, we don't trade every opportunity and have used our experience in this area to develop a set of criteria that each trade must meet before entry. If some of these criteria aren't met then we may still enter the trade but with a reduced position size or else we might avoid the trade altogether.

Basically, we only want to enter trades where we can limit our downside and where we have a reasonable prospect of making a profit via either an improved bid and/or some other special feature of the offer.

This strategy seems relatively simple in that we are just buying companies that are subject to a takeover but we have used this strategy for many years and it continues to be a consistent winner for us when used correctly.

The cherry on the cake: market neutrality

The massive advantage in trading takeovers, and why we love them so much, is that they are a market neutral strategy. What this means is that you don't have to predict market direction to make money using this strategy.

The market could go up 10%, it could go down 15% or it could trade sideways and in each instance will have a minimal effect on the outcome of each of our trades.

How many times have you woken up after a massive drop in US indices and thought to yourself "Oh no, my super fund is going to get smashed today?"

Imagine waking up and thinking "Wow our market is probably going to take a big hit today. Luckily it won't affect me." This is the big advantage of trading this particular strategy.

When a company announces a takeover, its share price is no longer influenced by day to day market fluctuations. Instead, the company's share price is determined by the probability of that offer being successful (in its current form or otherwise).

If the US market drops 5% overnight, as long as the conditions of the deal haven't changed then neither will the price of the company under takeover and nor should it.

This means that the volatility of your positions are significantly reduced and because of that you can sleep easy at night knowing it doesn't matter what happens, your stocks will be unaffected.

If you run a SMSF then we believe that you should seriously consider trading existing takeover bids to generate consistent profits in a low risk manner.

3.3 Buy-backs

Exploiting predetermined discounted rates

Another great low risk strategy to trade in your SMSF is to participate in certain company share buy backs.

When a company wants to return excess capital to its shareholders it may do so via a share buy-back.

When a company does a buyback it sets a date in the future (the Record Date) whereby all shareholders as of that date may sell some or all of their shares back to the company at a predetermined price. In most cases the price is at a slight discount to the current share price but includes a large fully franked dividend component. This inclusion of a fully franked dividend makes the opportunity extremely attractive to those people on low income tax rates and you guessed it, a SMSF!

In some cases it results in shareholders receiving a better after tax outcome than if they sold their shares on market. These are the opportunities we want to trade!

Let's look at an example to see how you can benefit from companies that announce a buy-back. Sometimes these deals can be quite complex so it is in your best interest to seek professional taxation advice so that you are aware of the exact benefits that you stand to receive when your personal tax situation is taken into account.

We are going to go out on a limb here and guess you have heard of Telstra (ASX Code: TLS).

In August 2014 Telstra announced that it was going to return some of its excess capital back to shareholders in the form of a share buyback.

This offer was announced to the market on the 14th of August 2014. To determine which shareholders would be eligible to participate, the company set a record date of 22nd of August 2014. What this meant was that if you weren't a current shareholder of Telstra you had until the 19th of August 2014 to acquire the shares so that you would qualify to participate in the buy-back.

You may be asking why the last day to buy shares was the 19th and not the record date of the 22nd. In order to qualify for the offer, your shares need to have settled and you must appear on the company's share register as at the 22nd. On the ASX, the settlement process takes 3 business days following the day upon which you purchased the shares, also known as T+3.

So if you buy shares on Tuesday 19th August (the last day to buy) it will take until Friday 22nd of August for the shares to settle.

The tricky bit...

Things are about to get a little tricky so it may pay to read through the section that follows several times until you can follow the mechanics.

TLS announced that the price that they were going to buy back the shares at (the 'Buy-Back Price') would be at a discount to the current market price. This 'Market Price' was to be the volume weighted average price (VWAP) of TLS over the five trading days leading up to and including the Buy-Back Closing Date of October 3rd 2014.

When tendering their shares into the buy-back, eligible shareholders needed to specify a discount amount that they were happy to tender their shares at. This discount had to be specified at a level between 6% and 14% below the 'Market Price' that would be calculated using the VWAP criteria above. TLS would then determine the percentage discount which would result in the maximum number of shares being bought back without exceeding the $1 billion dollar limit (i.e. the maximum value of shares that the company wished to buy back in aggregate).

Let's say that you decided that you wanted to tender your shares at an 8% discount to the market price. If Telstra calculated a final discount percentage that was greater than that, say 10%, then you would not have your shares bought back.

Alternatively you could elect to tender your shares at the final tender price meaning that your shares would be bought back regardless of the calculated discount determined by Telstra.

So, now you have become an eligible shareholder and decided on the percentage discount you are happy to tender your shares at, but what is the actual deal?

The buy-back had 2 components:

1. A capital component of $2.33 and

2. A fully franked dividend component equal to the difference between the final buy-back price and $2.33.

Considering the buyback price was not known at the time of purchasing the shares we would not know the exact benefit to be received in dollar terms until after the final buy-back price was announced on the 6th of October 2014. Obviously, the higher the final price the better as that would increase the dividend amount that we would receive and ultimately the franking credits we would also receive.

On the 6th of October, TLS announced that the 'Market Price' had been calculated to be $5.3418 and that the Buy-Back Price was set at a 14% discount to this price i.e. $4.60. The fact that the discount was set at the maximum 14% was always the likely outcome considering the extent to which the buy-back would be likely to appeal to Telstra's large number of retail shareholders (many of whom would likely have owned TLS via their SMSF – more on that below).

Which means?

So, what exactly does that outcome mean for those entities with a zero tax rate such as a super fund in the pension phase?

Shareholders would receive a capital component of $2.33 and a fully franked dividend of $2.27. Therefore the franking credit that investors would receive is $0.973.

Shareholders were also eligible, as part of this particular deal, for another separate fully franked final dividend of $0.15 that was paid on the 29th of August 2014. The franking credits attached to this dividend were $0.064.

Considering all of these components in aggregate, the total effective sale price of your TLS holding would have been $5.787.

If you purchased your shares on the day the buy-back was announced, you would have achieved an entry price between $5.49 and $5.58, depending on what time of the day you purchased your shares at.

If you purchased 925 shares, which was the maximum amount that you could purchase before scale back was applied to your holding, you would have made between $191.48 and $274.73 less trading costs. Not a massive profit by any means but one that was made whilst incurring very little risk and deploying very little capital. Exactly the type of trade that we are hoping to do as often as we possibly can.

This is just another example of a situation in which a little digging into the terms of a deal can result in very low risk profits and an example of a great strategy to utilize within your SMSF.

3.4 Dividends/franking credits

Free lunch!

We have left the best to last. You may have heard the saying 'there is no such thing as a free lunch'. In our opinion, the franking credits attached to many dividends are the closest thing to a 'free lunch' in the financial markets that you're likely to find. It's the gift to a SMSF (in particular) that just keeps on giving.

In an environment of low interest rates, money sitting in a bank account will yield little return with the typical 'high interest' account at an Australian bank currently paying interest of about 2.5% per annum, investors aren't exactly rushing to the bank to deposit large amounts of cash.

Instead investors are in search of alternatives that are relatively safe but offer higher returns. This is especially true at a time when the number of SMSFs are increasing at an exponential rate.

You may already know about the benefits of receiving fully franked dividends (we've touched on them already in this book). If you are familiar with the benefits, then you probably already know what we are about to share. For those readers who don't already know, fully franked dividends are very valuable to those people or entities who have a low marginal tax rate (**guess** who they are).

Fully franked dividends are payments made by a company from earnings that have already been taxed at the Australian company tax rate of 30%. What this means is that if you are on a tax rate that is lower than 30%, you should qualify for a tax credit for the amount of tax paid by the company that is in excess of the amount that you would otherwise have been required to pay (based on your marginal tax rate). This tax credit is known as a franking credit.

The ideal scenario would be if you have a SMSF that pays no tax. In that case you would be able to claim all of the franking credit back when you complete your tax return. If you are taxed at 15% (as a SMSF is in the accumulation phase) then you would be entitled to claim back half of the franking credit.

The rules to bear in mind

Obviously, everybody's situation is different and whether or not you can use franking credits to your advantage will depend on your personal tax situation, but there are a few rules you should be aware of if your marginal tax rate is lower than 30% as doing so can help you generate some easy money.

The first rule is what is commonly called the 45 day holding rule. This requires investors to hold their shares 'at risk' for a minimum of 45 days to receive the benefits of the franking credits. In simple terms, it means that you must hold a position that is not more than 30% hedged for 45 days (not including either the purchase or sale date) to be able to claim the tax credit potentially on offer.

There is an exemption to this rule that you need to be aware of though and that is that the 45 day rule does not apply where an individual investor's total franking credits do not exceed $5,000 during the financial year. What this means is that if you have accumulated less than $5,000 in franking credits during the year, you need not hold the shares 'at risk' for 45 days in order to claim the benefits of those franking credits.

Some dividends are fully franked and some can be partially franked meaning you can only claim a partial credit.

So how do you calculate the amount of franking credits and the amount that you have accumulated?

The formula for franking credit success

A simple formula can be used to determine the amount of franking credits that you have received from a dividend. This is:

$$\text{Franking credit} = \text{Dividend amount} \times 30/70$$

So assume you received a fully franked dividend of $120. The franking credit you will receive is $120 \times 30/70 = 51.42.

This is the portion of tax that has already been paid by the company on the profits it has paid to you as a dividend. So if you are a stay at home mum or dad and earn less than the tax free threshold (Currently $18,200) you can claim this amount in your tax return and receive a full refund of $51.42.

As discussed above, you can claim up to $5,000 worth of these credits and be exempt for the 45 day holding rule. So, if for example, the wife of a married couple works and the husband stays home to take care of the kids, it makes sense to buy shares in his name so that he can receive a refund for the full amount.

Please note that the dividend amount (excluding the franking credit) is classed as income so you need to take that into account when determining your assessable income.

Not everyone however is in this position. A zero tax rate is the ideal position to be in when claiming franking credits as you get the full amount back but it's not the only one.

As long as you have a tax rate of less than 30% you can still benefit from investing in a company paying fully franked dividends. You will only get a partial credit but it's better than nothing and still a great opportunity to make some easy money.

Many of the opportunities that we trade are chosen because they include franking credits. The two strategies that we went through above often include franking credits as part of the terms of the deal. In many cases the return you will make off the actual trade will be small (sometimes as low as 2%) but the trade-off is that they have a very high probability of success. What this means is that you essentially get the franking credits with little risk of losing the capital you've invested in the trade to begin with.

A yearly subscription to our service currently costs $990. If you only traded the opportunities we identify that include franking credits and were able to claim the full amount of the franking credits on offer you would well and truly cover the cost of your subscription and then some. Accumulating $5,000 worth of franking credits in any given year would pay for your annual subscription for over 5 years.

The point we are trying to make of course is that on the surface these types of trades may look like they generate an average return and are therefore often neglected by those who have overlooked the specifics of the trade. Those who dig a little deeper will find the gems hidden just below the surface.

CHAPTER 4

All in the mind - is psychology important?

Introduction

The markets are places of high excitement, fast movement, fleeting opportunities. They are also places where people are making decisions that have huge impact on their own, and their clients', financial well-being.

Emotions can run high. It's easy to get swept away.

But similarly, a level head can put you at a real advantage – and not just in terms of making sensible decisions with your own investments, but also in terms of learning to recognise conditions that might present opportunities born of other traders succumbing to emotional responses to market conditions.

In this chapter we will explore the impact of emotions on the market and how to keep a clear head in the heat of the moment:

1. **How do emotions affect business?**

    Excitement, Denial, Fear of Missing Out, Anger, Frustration, Panic and Despair – all emotions traders feel when watching their positions – but what is their impact on the market? And how do you plan to watch your own emotions?

2. **Changing your mindset**

    However the markets make you feel, a rational, analytical and dispassionate perspective will always yield the most appropriate response – but the only way to master you emotions is to practice doing so.

4.1 Do emotions affect my outcome?

A cool head

If you have traded previously you will know that there are some days when nothing you do goes right. You may have followed your system meticulously and then made a simple error that cost you your profits for the day – effectively undoing all of your hard work.

When trading it's important to keep a cool head, stay composed, and focus on the long term profitability of your trading and not the short term ups and downs. We are unaware of anyone who has been consistently profitable in trading the market whilst also being emotionally unstable!

Some in the industry claim that up to 95% of trading success (or failure) can be attributed to trading psychology. Not the system, not the software and not how much money you have!

Excitement, Denial, Fear of Missing Out, Anger, Frustration, Panic and Despair are all emotions that a trader may feel when watching their positions. Every day these emotions effect the share price of companies listed on world markets. When trading money that you need to live on in retirement emotions can be magnified even further.

There are individuals out there who have studied the effects that the interplay of these emotions have on the market and can spot opportunities that arise when less experienced traders overreact to a situation.

Resisting temptation

You often see a company come out with an announcement and the share price quickly shoots up 10% in response. Investors who experience the fear of missing out (FOMO) purchase shares for a price way above its fair value. They then experience anger when the share price then takes a sharp turn to the downside and erases the recent spike, and more. This is a very common occurrence!

Learning how to control your emotions is an important skill that can significantly improve your trading results but it's one of the hardest skills to master.

Sometimes we log in to the trading forum Hot Copper (an online forum for stock traders). We don't do this to find a next trade or to make investment decisions, but to observe the market from a psychological point of view.

A lot of investors on Hot Copper self-proclaim that they are long term investors only to then question why a stock has dropped 10% the next day. We can always tell who is experienced at trading and who is new to the market.

Those who have been trading for a long time and say that they are long term investors don't care about the day to day movements in the stock price. The stock could drop 50% (hopefully you don't experience a loss like this) and as long as the fundamentals haven't changed and their system hasn't triggered an exit they can maintain their composure as they are trading on the facts and not second guessing themselves over why they are still in the trade. They know that it's not their emotions that decides their entry and exits, it's their system that does that.

On the other hand the inexperienced investor sees a drop of 10% and starts to get concerned that they have missed something. They start to question themselves and ultimately end up exiting the stock prematurely. If the stock continues to drop they feel like they have made the right decision even though they have traded contrary to their system.

This is potentially more damaging than most people think as it will start to place seeds of doubt in your consciousness about the reliability of your system. Instead of trusting the way you trade you will now think "well I closed the last trade early and I was right." Pretty soon you aren't following any system and start to trade based solely on your emotions. This is a dangerous place to be and one that you must try to avoid at all costs.

4.2 Controlling your mindset

Be a scientist – not an artist

To trade effectively you almost have to become a robot with no emotions. As humans we are emotional by nature. If we have a good day and make a good profit we become ecstatic and happy with ourselves. When we have a bad day or make an error we become angry and start to question our ability as a trader.

The hardest thing to do as a trader is to eliminate emotional behaviour and trade with a clear mind. Some people find this easier to do than others but when you finally gain the ability, trading becomes a lot easier.

Early on in our careers we used to be a victim to this type of behaviour. We felt over the moon when we made substantial profits but on the flip side felt disappointment when we lost money. After years of practice and consistently trading our system we are now able to (largely) separate our emotions from trading so much so that our family and friends would be hard pressed to tell at day's end whether we had experienced a profitable day or a losing one.

If we have a good day we now put it out of our mind and focus back on finding the next opportunity. Conversely we do the same if we have had a bad day. This process allows us to think long term and not be distracted by day to day movements of our portfolio.

There is no simple fix to stop your emotions affecting your trading. It would be good if we had a switch on the side of our heads that allowed us to turn them off and on as we saw fit but unfortunately that isn't the case. With time you will learn to control yourself and trade with a calm clear manner at all times - it won't happen overnight but it will happen.

Holding your nerve in the face of loss

Most people don't have an issue with the winning side of things but they often have a problem with losing. No one likes losing money but unfortunately it's a big part of trading and one that cannot be avoided. In order to make it in the market you need to get used to making a loss and accept that it is a part of the game.

There have been numerous studies done that suggest that losing money is twice as painful as the joy of a corresponding gain. That is, we feel considerably more grief about a $100 loss than we do happiness about a $100 windfall.

A study by Daniel Kahneman and Amos Tversky found that people's attitudes toward risks concerning gains was quite different from their attitudes toward risks concerning losses.

For example, when given a choice between getting $1,000 with certainty and having a 50% chance of getting $2,500 they may well choose the certain $1,000 in preference to the uncertain chance of getting $2,500 even though the mathematical expectation of the uncertain option is $1,250.[5]

This is a perfectly reasonable attitude that is described as risk-aversion. But Kahneman and Tversky found that the same people when confronted with a certain loss of $1,000 versus a 50% chance of no loss or a $2,500 loss often choose the risky alternative. This is called risk-seeking behaviour.

A helpful activity to speed up your progress is to monitor your emotional state when entering and exiting trades. Keeping an emotion journal can also help. If you become aware of when you are overly happy or angry you can take steps to change that state and bring yourself back to a calm controlled state. Over time this will become second nature and you will find yourself automatically returning to a neutral state without even thinking about it.

---

5   http://www.sjsu.edu/faculty/watkins/prospect.htm

EPILOGUE

Putting it all into practice - a day in our life

Introduction

Here we are going to do something that is rarely done. We will go through exactly what we do on a daily basis. Our method is different to most in that we trade on company announcements. We rarely enter a trade from a technical standpoint when trading takeovers. We do use technical analysis to identify our stops and therefore determine our position size (according to our pre-set risk amount). However, if you are a technical trader (or planning to be) and determine your entry signals based on charting patterns, your day will be different.

How we are set up

To start we will run through the systems that we use to trade. This will give you an idea of what a professional uses to try and give them an advantage in the market. Currently we use Intel i5 processors running a 3.33 GHz processor and 6GB RAM. Chad has a 4 screen setup running the 64 bit version of windows 7. Luke uses a similar setup but runs a 6 screen setup so he can monitor more stocks at the same time.

The speed of our computers is not as critical as it would be for someone who day trades. For a day trader, they need to enter and exit trades quickly and even a 1 second delay can be the difference between a winning trade and a losing trade. The trades that we typically trade are not usually time sensitive. There are instances where speed is critical and we need to enter a trade quickly which is why we have reasonably fast computers but in most cases the opportunity will be around for days and sometimes longer. So don't worry, you could trade the opportunities we trade with the Pentium computer you bought in 2001 provided it doesn't crash in the midst of you placing a trade!

In terms of the programs we use, most are available to anyone wanting to give trading a shot. Some however are expensive to run and therefore not financially viable for the typical investor.

For trading we use E*TRADE Australia and also IG markets. We have accounts with both of these brokers so that we have access to the instruments we need. If you trade futures or direct US equities you may need an account with a broker such as Interactive Brokers who offers trading in those instruments.

For charting and market analysis we use an institutional version of IRESS. This provides us with real time information on everything from stock prices, company announcements and sector indices. This costs us around $1,000 a month for each licence and we have 2. This is one program you probably won't need and probably won't have access to as it is not available to retail clients. It is however one of the most reliable systems available which is why we pay so much for it. You can get a cut down version at lesser cost but even so, unless you are very active and profitable enough to justify the cost it's probably not worth paying for.

As a charting package we use Beyond Charts that is produced by Share Wealth Systems and have subscriptions to almost every news service in Australia. For us news is a major key to our success.

What a typical day looks like

At 8am (or before) we will start the day by looking at what happened overnight in international markets. Although our trading is unaffected by these moves as discussed before, we still have an interest in the markets so it's helpful to know what is happening around the world.

On the way into the office Chad is usually on Twitter looking for anything that may be worthy of closer inspection. Most of it is just people posting useless junk but he can quiet often find something that is interesting. Luke starts his day by reading the Australian Financial review over breakfast and so too The New York Times, The Financial Times, The Wall Street Journal, several blogs and Australia's other major newspapers.

Luke will do a review of all our positions held by 789 Asset Management (our hedge fund entity) and make sure that there are no updates that we have to report or take action on.

Most of our day is spent reading and we spend a lot of time doing it. We can't stress this enough. We have proprietary tools including macro driven excel spreadsheets and news alerts that we have built to help us identify articles that may be of use but we still have to do the leg work. Just like technical traders who use charts and a combination of indicators to identify trades, our indicators are company announcements and news articles.

There are no shortcuts to finding the opportunities in these reports. Yes we can use our experience to look at a specific section of the announcement to find potential trades but if it looks like a good opportunity we will read the entire document to make sure that there aren't any hidden clauses that could ruin the trade.

After market we do another review of our positions and catch up on any articles or announcements that we may have missed during the day.

We rarely take a day off when the market is open and make sure that if one of us is away the other is here to cover. Our biggest fear is that if we miss a day, that day could be the one where a significant opportunity presents itself and not being in the office would mean that we were unable to take advantage of it. Our subscribers don't pay us to miss those opportunities (and nor do the clients of our hedge fund) and we work hard to make sure that we are up to date with any good trading opportunities that meet our pre-determined criteria.

The market is an extremely competitive environment. If you are serious about a career in trading or making money in the market then we can tell you that it is more than a full time job. You need to commit everything you can into making that happen and if you can't do that then you should be looking for someone who can do so successfully on your behalf.

Conclusion

So there you have it. If you are already trading via a SMSF we hope the information that we have covered in this book has been useful. If you are not already trading in a SMSF we hope that we have given you reason to consider doing so in future.

Trading doesn't have to be a risky endeavour and you don't have to fear the market. There are simple ways (that almost seem too simple) to make money in the market. Sometimes you just need some support to gain the confidence to trade them.

We hope we have given you some of that confidence.

GLOSSARY

A summary of key terms - knowledge is power

KeyTerms

Short Selling - The sale of a security that is not owned by the seller, or that the seller has borrowed. Short selling is motivated by the belief that a security's price will decline, enabling it to be bought back at a lower price to make a profit.

SMSF - Self-managed super fund.

Takeover - When one company makes an offer to buy all assets of another company.

IPO - An "Initial Public Offering" is the first sale of stock by a private company to the public.

Buy-back - The repurchase of outstanding shares (repurchase by a company in order to reduce the number of shares on the market.

Limit order - An order to purchase a security at or below a specified price (or to sell at or above a specified price).

Market order - An order that an investor makes through a broker or brokerage service to buy or sell an investment immediately at the best available current price.

Day trader - This involves buying and subsequently selling financial instruments within the same trading day, such that all positions will usually be closed before the market close of the trading day.

Swing trader - A style of trading that attempts to capture gains in a stock within one to four days. Swing traders use technical analysis to look for stocks with short-term price momentum.

Long term investor - This involves buying shares and holding them for long term growth. Generally over a number of years.

Volatility - Refers to the amount of uncertainty or risk about the size of changes in a security's value.

Leveraged products - A facility that enables you to gain a large exposure to a financial market while only tying up a relatively small amount of your capital.

Market neutral - A strategy whereby the trader's profitability isn't linked to a market direction and they can therefore achieve a profitable outcome regardless of future moves in a security.

Risk management - A two-step process determining what risks exist in an investment and then handling those risks in a way best-suited to your investment objectives.

Compound returns - The rate of return, usually expressed as a percentage, that represents the cumulative effect that a series of gains or losses have on an original amount of capital over a period of time.

Hedging - A hedge is an investment position intended to offset potential losses/gains that may be incurred by a companion investment.

Mechanical trading system - Buying and selling stocks according to a set of predetermined criteria, usually technical indicators such as relative strength or momentum.

VWAP - The Volume Weighted Average Price(VWAP) is calculated by adding up the dollars traded for every transaction (price multiplied by number of shares traded) and then dividing by the total shares traded for the day.

Drawdown - The peak-to-trough decline during a specific record period of an investment, fund or commodity. A drawdown is usually quoted as the percentage between the peak and the trough.

Franking credit - A franking credit is a nominal unit of tax paid by companies using dividend imputation. Shareholders include in their assessable income not the dividends received but the grossed-up amount back-calculated from that dividend and the current tax rate, then have their income tax payable calculated thereupon, then use franking credits to offset tax payable at the rate of a dollar per credit.

45 Day Holding Rule - The 45 day holding period rule requires investors to hold their shares "at risk" for a minimum of 45 days to receive the benefits of franking credits.

Full service broker - A broker that provides a large variety of services to its clients, including research and advice, retirement planning, tax tips, and much more.

Market depth - A measure of the number of open buy and sell orders for a security or currency at different prices. The depth of market measure provides an indication of the liquidity and depth for that security or currency.

Technical analysis - Is a security analysis methodology for forecasting the direction of prices through the study of past market data, primarily price and volume.

Fundamental analysis - A method of evaluating a security that entails attempting to measure its intrinsic value by examining related economic, financial and other qualitative and quantitative factors.

Backtesting - The process of testing a trading strategy on prior time periods. Instead of applying a strategy for the time period forward, which could take years, a trader can do a simulation of his or her trading strategy on relevant past data in order to gauge the its effectiveness.

Forward testing - Is the simulation of the real markets data on paper only. It means that though you are moving along the markets live, but you are not actually putting in real money, but doing virtual trading in live markets to understand the movements of markets better.

Market scanning software - A program used to find opportunities in the market based on your chosen parameters.

Static data - A snapshot of data at that specific time. New data needs to be accessed regularly in order to be kept up to date

Real time data - Updates automatically without the need for the user to manually request new data.

Risk seeking - Is a person who has a preference for risk

Risk aversion - Is the reluctance of a person to accept a bargain with an uncertain payoff rather than another bargain with a more certain, but possibly lower, expected payoff. For example, a risk-averse investor might choose to put his or her money into a bank account with a low but guaranteed interest rate, rather than into a stock that may have high expected returns, but also involves a chance of losing value.

www.ingramcontent.com/pod-product-compliance
Lightning Source LLC
Chambersburg PA
CBHW072306200526
45168CB00014B/870